Trim Reckonings

DeWitt Henry

From Shylock to the hucklebuck (the dance craze of his adolescence) to an epic "Funky Robot," DeWitt Henry's poems are openhearted, witty, often rueful, in loving argument with literature and with what it means to be human—and with meaning itself. Profound and often profoundly, wryly funny, *Trim Reckonings* asks questions poems don't seem to have asked before, and leaves this reader in wonder.

Gail Mazur
Author of *Land's End: New and Selected Poems*

In this stunning new collection, DeWitt Henry reckons with a past that is personal, familial, and cultural as well as the present dysfunction of American political life. His narratives and portraits are drawn and colored by candid and resonant observations. Henry is a poet who both sees the larger landscape and the struggles of the individual figures at play within it. Additionally, Henry draws upon his insights into literary figures and their characterizations, for *Trim Reckonings* is a reader's reckoning as well as a writer's! These are hard-won, earned, poems of passionate engagement.

Stuart Dischell
Author of *The Lookout Man*

"Are scars proof of wounds / or of healing?" So asks DeWitt Henry's splendid second book of poems, *Trim Reckonings*. The personal family drama of Henry's youth—adultery, alcoholism, disappointments—is set against the historical backdrop of the post-WW II America. The funny tumble and tumult of objects and heirlooms—a dismantled German gas mask, a clear plastic Nixon Halloween mask, a carved coconut pirate head, a collapsible top hat, each one evokes (for me) a memory and a revelation. They are not just a stroll through nostalgia's flea market but are uncanny and relevant under Henry's witty gaze. These primarily meditative poems are presented as jazzy, charged, inventive, literary riffs, yet one can see through the delightful verbal high-jinx and sleight-of-hand surfaces to the darker subjects underneath—the "scars" (psychological and historical) that are the anchor and the heart of this rich collection.

Jane Shore
Author of *That Said*

First Edition, First Printing — November 2023
Library of Congress Control Number: 2023931016
ISBN 978-1-953136-42-8   Hardback
ISBN 978-1-953136-41-1   Paperback
ISBN 978-1-953136-68-8   Audiobook

Cover Art by **Pierian Springs Press**
Cover Design by **Kurt Lovelace**
Cover type *Bauhaus Dessau* **Alfarn** by Céline Hurka,
Elia Preuss, Flavia Zimbardi,
Hidetaka Yamasaki, and Luca Pellegrini.
Poetry title and body set in *URW* **Baskerville**.
Misc. in **Jenson** by Robert Slimbach & **Sabon** by Jan Tschichold.
Flourishes set in Emigre Foundry **Dalliance**, by Frank Heine &
Emigre Foundry **ZeitGuys**, by Bob Aufuldish, Eric Donelan.
Typefaces licensed Adobe, Linotype, & URW GmbH.

PSPress.Pub
Pierian Springs Press, Inc
30 N Gould St, Ste 30
Sheridan, Wyoming 82801

For Connie, again

Part Four

Part Five

Part Six

"What is *honour?* a word. What is in that word
honour? what is that *honour?* air. A trim reckoning!"

Falstaff, HENRY IV, PART I

Trim Reckonings

DeWitt Henry

PART ONE

Gas Mask

After my Uncle John
returned from the Battle of the Bulge,
he claimed he never killed anyone,
but had been shot at.
He brought home trophies approved by his superiors:
a 9mm Luger pistol
and a fluted, dark green metal
canister with a swastika on the lid.

He let my oldest brother
(a hunter, but too young
to draft) fire the Luger once,
which otherwise he kept
in a special drawer. However,
the canister, with its shoulder-strap,
thumb-lever catch, and rubber mask
folded inside, was his gift to us.

The eyes were round lenses;
a thick, round can screwed onto
the mouth-hole, like a car!s oil filter.
The mask fit over your face, with straps
around your head, and made you sweat.
In war, a helmet would go on top.

My brothers took turns
wearing it for Halloween.
They let me try it on, but
my head was too small.
I didn't like the smell,
the clouded lenses and heave
of each breath. Imagine gas,
like being under water!

In time, the mask itself was
thrown out, stolen, or lost,
but I kept the canister
for cap-guns and other toys.

Medallion

Our family kept heirlooms
both obvious and strange.
Coconut pirate heads
with bandanas and wooden
daggers in their teeth.
A polar bear-skin rug.
A collapsable top hat.

But most fascinating was
a gold medallion, with
a photograph of my mother,
posed and colorized,
and mounted under glass.
She kept it on her desk.
I had never seen her
with dark hair,
so young, so beautiful.

I was nine when she left
alone for a "vacation"
(we'd never been separated).
I fell sick with a fever
and begged my older sister
to bring me the medallion,
which I lifted from its case
and kissed, then pressed against
my cheeks, feeling how cool
the metal was. Soon after
—days, not weeks—she filled
my doorway, rushed in,
and gathered me in arms.

For my mother, the medallion
had been an artifact of vanity,
taken before the births
of my brothers and sister;
before my father's drink and adultery;
before her own broken dreams.

During her absence, she had
decided to stay with the marriage,
she explained; I was the writer,
home from college. I'd begun
researching our family story
and asked to see the medallion.

My sister, in her mid-eighties,
divorced, house-ridden,
and a continent away,
remains the medallion's keeper
for her daughters and grandsons.

Masquers

given our father's sudden death
transparent Halloween masks
protected me,
my older brothers, and sister
from grief, or its lack

my mother had called us home
to Villanova, Pennsylvania
from distant lives
in California, Massachusetts,
New Jersey and Colorado

after the funeral,
we took a break, just sibs,
to get more cigarettes or ice,
and tour familiar streets
until we stopped on impulse
at the local toy store,
a mecca of our youths
now stocked for Halloween

clear plastic masks
were our find, and hit;
eerie how our skins
showed through, with
features changed

We wore them on the way back,
taking turns and laughing.
JFK, Johnson, Nixon, Ford.
Each mask looked different
on a different wearer.

Then home with Mom
our spouses disapproved,
given the occasion.
What were we thinking?

But Mom reached for
my Nixon mask, slipped it on,
shook her head, made V signs;
growled: "I'm not a crook!"

Pratfalls

Your middle brother Chuck
promised to catch you.
He'd practiced himself
with your oldest brother Jack.

Remember? Stand straight,
face him. Hands at sides.
Shoulders back. Tuck chin.
lean forward, like a board.
Don't catch yourself or step.
No hands out. Just topple.

You try, but take a saving step.
"Don't worry. We'll try it again!
I'll catch you. Promise."

You do, this time. He does:
inches from the ground.

We made an act of it.
Not only on backyard grass,
or rug inside, but on
our swimming club's cement,
while others stared.

That's love, he said.
That's faith.

(That's life, I think now,
both for clowns and
children of alcoholics.)

Scars

Three inches under my jaw, right side,
where at age five,
I had surgery
(my sister remembers),
for an infected lymph node.

One inch, left hand
between little and ring fingers,
where I got cleated
in high school football.

Four inches, left elbow,
from fixing a barbed wire fence
on a ranch before college.

Thirty-five years of running
ended in a bad fall from a curb,
surgery for "bilateral complete
quad tendon rupture,"
and eight-inches on both knees.

*

But *nothing* in my life
equals my father's scar.

As a teen, he'd had osteomyelitis
in his left femur. A groove
of infected marrow had been
taken, leaving his leg
permanently weakened
and a deep crevice, hip to knee,
where folds of the incision
had grown into the bone.

He limped. He fell away
on his right leg with his golf swing.
He rarely went swimming.
I was squeamish at the sight.
And when, age seven, I ran
for his protection
from thunder and lightning,
and he welcomed me into
his bed, I was afraid,
somehow, of bumping against
or falling into the scar.

*

I have my invisible ones:
disappointed heart;
failures, faults, betrayals
of myself and others;
stupidities and shame.
Losses of loved ones.

But *nothing* like my father's
breakdown before I was born,
his alcoholic "bad times,"
which left him odd, brooding,
and beholden to my mother.
"She stuck with me through it all,"
he marveled, the one time
he told me his version.
"Most women wouldn't have.
She's one woman in a thousand."

*

Are scars the proof of wounds
or of healing?

*

"Tribal Scars" I called my
memoir after his death,
but a friend warned me
that no one would buy
a book with "scars" in its title,

So I decided on "Sweet Dreams."

PART TWO

On Charm

In manners, grace, and accent,
  such as Southern charm,
"Come again, y'all." Or Irish,
"Sure'n top of the mornin' t'ya!"
  English: "Charmed, I'm sure."
"Enchante" (French). "Mucho gusto" (Spanish).
  Greeks, bearing gifts.

Or in magic.

She led a charmed life,
as if a St. Christopher dangled
from her rearview.
Charm bracelets. Rabbit feet.

Behold the snake charmer.
"Musick has Charms to sooth a savage Breast,
  To soften Rocks, or bend a knotted Oak,"
wrote William Congreve.

Charms can be malicious too.
Siren songs. Voodoo dolls staked.
Slaughtered chickens. Poisoned apples.
Scottish witches with their stew:
"cool the mixture with baboon blood.
  After that the charm is finished."

Bodegas offer supplies
both for curse and remedy.
Wizards battle spell vs. spell.

Prince Charming's kiss
awakens Sleeping Beauty.

Alfred Kazin dissed J. D. Salinger
for relying more on charm
than vision, for being
"consciously appealing and
consciously clever" with his Glasses,
as if nostalgia for innocence
could save a fallen world.

Shakespeare's Perdita
is never "cute," yet raised as
a shepherdess, she enchants
the young, old, rural, and worldly,
and all her acts are queens.

Natural charms or nurtured?
Charm offensive. Charm school.
Mi casa es su casa.

Strippers' body parts—e.g.
her cheekbones (high), lips (full), T&A (ample);
or *his* jaw (square), abs (washboard), biceps (bugling),
glutes (tight)—are charms, aka assets.
As is wealth. According to Gatsby,
Daisy's voice was "full of money."

Yet charm lacks glamor's power;
suggests diversions and appeals
more modest than stunning.

For poems themselves as charms,
see Old English "Against Wens":
"Clinge þu   alsƿa col on heorþe,
scring þu   alsƿa scerne aƿage";[1]
Spenser's "Epithalamion"
in lieu of many ornaments;
Frost's momentary stay.

---

[1] trans.: "Shrivel as the coal upon the hearth! Shrink as the muck in the stream…"

On Drift

To coast gently, to move.
You get my drift,
meaning: meaning.
In air, for birds, planes,
balloons and kites,
a plastic grocery bag.
Grief lanterns, rising.
Clouds too, very like whales.
Canoe with current.
Snow drifts, sand drifts,
windblown and sculpted.
Falling leaf pirouettes.
Drift wood. Smoke.
Unchained melodies
distant voices or song,
odors of barbecue.
Drifters, unmoored,
or aimless; wanderers.
Cast adrift.
Drift apart.
Thoughts drift.
Eye motes. Continents.
Plates riding magma.
Drift off course.
Cut motor, drift to stop.
Drift to sleep.

On Risk

Nothing ventured/gained. Never up/in. Risk tolerance (with investments). Risk free (offer). Risk ready? Win your life by losing it. Pregnant or not? HIV? STD? Fasten your seatbelt. Hazmat suits. Latex gloves. Smoking may be dangerous to your health. The most dangerous game. High risk sports, where the point is not to die. Russian roulette (one loaded, five empty). Credit score. Life insurance (all insurance). Actuarial odds. Warranties. Liability waivers. No lifeguards, swim at risk. Thrill rides. Sure things. Head in sand. Bomb shelters or swimming pools? Risk in writing. Hedging bets. Playing safe. Over your head. Shooting the works. Hope for best, brace for worst. Evel Knievel. Fools rush in. Hamlet follows the ghost.

Macbeth jumps the life to come. Along the glass bridge, tourists crawl. We marry, we dare to have children ("What he [Levin] felt towards this little creature…was a new torture of apprehension"). We move to new worlds and jobs. Tempted, we risk our proper good.

Frost's dare not to care. Roads less travelled by. The unknown for the known. Familiar for strange. Calculated or senseless. Drop your guard. Trust your gut. Caution to winds.

Brave the elements. Set it free. One wild and precious life. Living is so dear.

On Heart

"The human heart," we say, meaning not only
blood-pumper (distinct from that of other species),
but also seat of emotions, conscience, compassion,
courage, appetite, tenacity, devotion. She or he has heart.
For he was great of heart. Her heart was
as big as the whole outdoors. Don't lose heart.
Heart stopping news. Heart in your mouth. Heart-sick.
Faint heart. In the heart of the heart of the country.
Heart-felt (sincere). Cheatin' heart. False heart. Heartless.
My heart is turned to stone. I strike it and it hurts my hand.
Hard heart. Soft. Bleeding heart. Heart of the matter. Core.
She had my heart as I had hers. Cold hearted. Down-hearted.
Seat of the soul (first organ to develop in the fetus).

Meaning too much, can "heart" mean anything at all?

I turned into a hart and my desires, like fell and cruel hounds,
E'er since pursue me. Your heart's desire. Heart of gold. You
and you are heart and heart. I heart New York. Heart rate.
Blood pressure. Heart broken. Take my heart in your hand.
I pledge allegiance, hand over heart (vowing on life itself).
Give me your heart. After my own heart. Heart strings.
Wear my heart on my sleeve for daws to peck at.
Heart throb. Heartache. Heart to heart. On, me hearties.
Learning by heart. Heart vs. Head. Eat your heart out.
Stolen heart. A heart unfortified.
Half- or full-hearted. Cleft in twain. Hearts in bellies.
Face without a heart. Vampire's staked.

Heads Up

Fathead, hothead, featherhead
headdress?), swelled head,
head in clouds, egg head, pinhead,
bull head, head-strong, lost head,
heads-on (theory), hands-on (practice).

Head vs. heart vs. belly:
which rules the body politic?

Heads or tails? Heads up!
Keep your head down. Get ahead.
Head off at the pass. Head start.
Head for head of the class.

Butt heads. Go head to head.
Two-heads better than one
(undecided, or carnival freak?).
Head over heels. Over my head.

Take me to your leader. Gotta go!
Where's the head? Headline.
Head waters. Head of Charles Regatta.

Get up full head of steam.
Heady. Guinness foam.
Good head on her shoulders.

Take a new heading, mark!
Know where you're headed.
Headlong. Headstrong.

Can't get you out of my head.
Going out of my head.
Sick in the head? See a shrink.

Hard head, gone soft.
Nod for yes, shake for no.
Off with hers! Axeman or guillotine?

Headhunter's (shrunken or hired).
Crush snake's under foot
unless it serves Athena.

Death's head. All in your head.
Live in your head. Head for words.

Empty head. Off the top of.
Took the top off. Turned mine.
Can't get you out of.

Any headway? Eyes in back of.
Going out of. Sometimes horned:
cuckold, stag, or devil.

Sometimes ass's, like Bottom's
(or up my own, talking shit).

So fast it could make
yours spin. I could do this
while standing on my head.

What's that in the road, ahead?
Bowed, up, or tilted back. Headrest.
Head-first or jump. Buried in sand.

On Rocks

Slept like one,
once lava,
now of ages.

Steady as, hard.
Split by lichen,
water flow or chisel.

Stoned, stoner.
Bone-breaker. Rolling.
Candy. Cocaine.

Wall, path, plinth;
face, quarry,
and foundation.

Testicles. Jewels.
Engagement ring.
Alcatraz. Gibraltar.

First tools.
Climber and jock.
Beats scissors, not paper.

Statue's flesh.
Forest petrified.
Idea fixed.

Alternative to hard place.
Shipwreck, marriage, vodka.
Third from sun.

No relation to motion,
such as earthquake,
music's wild beat,

or cradle's calm,
chorus line kicking,
thrusters towards stars.

The Real Thing

"Poets are...always sticking their emotions
   in things that have no emotions."
        J.D. Salinger, *"Teddy"*

1.

Instance: this classic Coke bottle. Empty. A twelve-ounce glass container, tinted green, with fluted contours like a hobble skirt, and tapering to a neck and mouth. Not a milk bottle. Not a beer bottle. Not a container for orange juice, tomato juice, or Gatorade. Not a even a bottle for other carbonated soft drinks. One of millions in space and in time, created in one of hundreds of glass bottle factories around the world, it has been standardized by molds, themselves standardized. This bottle, this very bottle, empty as it stands on the table before me, here in my kitchen, in Watertown, Massachusetts, in 2017, could be interchanged in space and time, past or future. It has that permanence, unchanged from some other bottle, say, in my youth, on some other table in 1948, in Philadelphia, empty now where I have placed it. Or this bottle might be indistinguishable from a bottle my son's unborn son might place down on some kitchen table years after my death, years after even my memory as ceased to be a conscious presence to my son. But interchangeable is not identical. This bottle is this bottle, here, now.

2.

The green upsets me. The tint of thick glass. The distortions of light, magnifying and containing the kitchen shapes around it. The pattern itself, familiar yet distant, closed and invariable. The fluted sides, the grooves, formed by what force? Ordained. The machined scrawl, cursive, of the logo. "Coca Cola," precise regardless of scale, here, on billboards, in the sky. The C and C like tidal waves. The bottle neck, constricting. Lips cold. The green of endings, illness, menace -- unnatural casts of brightness under churning skies.

3.

Alas, poor Coke! Quite empty? Where be your syrups now? Your sugars? Where your caffeine? Melancholy Coke, the lips have vanished that have known you. Twelve full ounces, long since drained, the gulper too, and spirit's quench.

4.

Curved below, curved above. Nestles to the grasping hand. Grace to these curves, long and lickable up the surface of smooth glass. Between the crevices. Smooth letters of the raised logo, raised like scars. The tapering neck. The round bulges, ridges, then convex bracelet, then ridge and curved opening. Shaped for lips. Shaped for sucking. Shaped for probing with the tongue. And plentitude. The once and future Coke, the omnipresent Coke. The readily available. The promise of relief. Of solace. My hand craves the feel. The sliding down into that finger closing grip. So mine. Spinning now like Fortune's wheel, it slows and stops and points at you, at me!

5.

Breakable. Smash-able. The smug form, thick glass. Designer detritus. As fixed and self satisfied as the glacier of enterprise, a glacier all of glass, of millions of bottles, like atoms, mounted and fused and flowing to the next global catastrophe. Formula coke. Sweet. Fizzy. Slight caffeine tag. Cocoa beans. Same caffeine in chocolate and coffee. Addiction. Third world addicts. Rotted teeth. Poor white trash. Bottles, bottles. Vending machine. Bottles. Bottles ranked and ready like cannon shelves. Next round into the chamber. Bottles like glass babies, pulled from wombs. Caps off! Flicked off. Cutting edges. Bottles fizzing, bottles exploding. The spew of fizz. Shaken secretly like bombs. Carbonation gas. Builds and builds, first pry and spews, fumes, spills, sticky everywhere. Bottles thrown. Smash on the wall.

Smash on street. Neck like a handle, wielded. Swinging. Smash again smash. Smithereens. The bottle tossed, cartwheeling over end, arcs high. Bottles against bottles. The glacier mass. The bottles on a fence, like crows set up, so pert, so hour glass, the handgun wavers, v sight, barrel sight, the bottle sits and wavers, one with sights, my breathing, tightening, can't control, the desperation, now, exploding, leap and instant crash, of glass, of dust. Of vanishing. The power. Pleasure. Need for that. Pleasure too in shards. The base intact. A fragment, like a piece of puzzle, "Coke."

6.

Curves of joy. Old friend. Familiar as this face. This hand. Quencher of thirst. Bringer of relief. The roundness. Communion. Share with me. One Coke for all mankind! Homey! All races, all cultures, all climes, all times, the human chain snakes infinite, singing, Cokes held high. No identity like yours. The flow of you. The grace. The fullness leading to supply.

Beneficence. Bottle of plenty. Forever ready, constant, your crisp and bubbly taste (vanilla, cinnamon, lavender, nutmeg, coriander, citrus with sugar and phosphoric acid), the guarantees of water, milk.

PART THREE

On Blurred Words

"Change the narrative" has
   trickled down from lit theory
   to news anchors, PR pros,
   and politicians. Perhaps they mean
   (to mean) "the perception of reality"
   as well as "changing the story to fit
   a self-serving truth." All stories,
   whether news or fiction, bear
   their teller's messages. "Optics"
   also emphasizes "appearances."
   Reality (whether staged or not)
   is distorted by camera lenses
   (whether photo, film, TV or iPhone;
   wide-angle, filtered, 360 degree,
   closeup, tele-or microscopic).

   Prescription lenses correct
   blurred vision, but blur for 20/20's.
   Funhouse mirrors distort, as do
   rose-colored glasses and 3-D
   throw-aways. VR goggles
   convince our eyes of a mirage
   we know to be mirage.

   The narrator, unless "unreliable,"
   has more "power" than the people
   he or she is telling about.
   Optics become opinions.

   Specialists "interrogate" stories
   to detect whether they are "toxic"
   (meaning as poisonous
   to culture as Love Canal
   to the environment).

The moral of W.S.'s
King Lear was revised to suit
Enlightenment tastes by Nahum Tate—
a Hollywood ending before
there was Hollywood.

Erich Fromm's psychoanalytic
reading of Little Red Riding Hood
sees the teller as a midwife, who
punishes the wolf's pregnancy envy
by having the huntsman
deliver Red and grand-mom,
replace them with stones,
and drown the wolf.

Critics point out that
in Disney films of the past decade
family rather than romantic love
is what saves us in the end.

This way, folks,
to Babel and its tower!

Fake Nudes

Mannequins wait for
the window dresser.

Dancers wear flesh-colored bodysuits
("is classical ballet ready
to embrace flesh tone tights?"
asked Dance Magazine in 2020).

Marble statuary.
Medieval humbling.
Renaissance glorification.

Breaking nudes.
All the nudes fit to print,
air-brushed in Playboy
but not in Penthouse.
Want the bad nudes first or the good?
For artist's model, see Jacques Rivette's
La Belle Noiseuse (1991), where
Emmanuelle Beart is forced to hold
poses that defy flesh.
"It's not about the flesh. Not about nudity,"
the artist's wife explains.

Compare eighty-year-old Lear's
"Off, off you lendings"
to King Tut's send-off,
dressed to the nines.

Inflatable sex dolls
for the affluent.

Professional bodies
topless on South Beach.
Strippers at work.

Nudism itself, insisting
that skin is natural,
nothing to hide.
Shame on squares who stare.

Except for the clinical gaze,
for health's sake.
Or airport body scans,
seeking weapons.

And the real? Best
recognized with eyes wide shut.
One flesh. Bared hearts.

On Invalid

Valid means strong, sound, whole,
still in force, capable, able-bodied;
as opposed to disabled, handicapped,
broken, rejected, expired. If it's
invalid send it back; repair, recycle;
rehabilitate, fix, renew. If infirm,
try the infirmary. To be invalidated
is to become as worthless as
Confederate cash, a bad check,
Samson shorn, fool's gold. Will is infinite
but execution limited. To be validated,
we're confirmed, credit good,
talent proven, subscription paid.
Powers, value and valor certified.
He ain't heavy, father, he's my brother.

On Fits

Our mechanic's hands
are sometimes too big for the
crevices of our Honda FIT.
We love its longevity, however,
and keep it fit with oil changes
and TLC; are surprised by how
many passengers and goods
squeeze in and how it squeezes
too into small parking spaces
at my gym, "Forever Fit"—especially
at crowded times, when parkers
prize spaces near the door and
are fit to be tied if forced to walk.

Consider the misfit Alice,
too big or small, eating this, drinking that
to fit through tiny doors or outgrow
a house from inside, bursting its seams.
Luckily her clothes grew or shrank with her.

The camel shies at needle's eye.
Elasticity proves fittest
for mice and octopi.
One size fits all,
transcending custom markets,
just as the adjustable wrench
or person for all seasons.

Fit to rule? To serve the public trust?
If the shoe fits, wear it, Cindy.
Job fits the fittest.

"Now does he feel his title
    hang loose about him,
    like a giant's robe
    upon a dwarfish thief."

"All the news that's fit to print,"
    vowed NYT owner, Aldolph S. Ochs
    in 1897, referring less to space
    than to decency, credibility and proof,
    as opposed to the yellow journalism of
    the Hearst and Pulitzer papers.

    No need for tailors.
    Missing pieces fall in place.

    The poet's Mind and World
    each fitted to the other,
    create with blended might,
    Wordsworth sang to
"fit audience though few."

On Comparison

Without it, no growth.
Marks on the doorjamb
for granddaughters' heights
at 3, 6, 10. You (me) then, and now:
our lives' prides, scars.

No comparing apples and
oranges, ducklings and swans.

Beware imitation, let alone
forgery, impersonation, parody.

Beware also envy or guilt,
measuring your lot by others.'

No boasting about wealth or pedigree.
No "lowering the basement."

Beware self-hate as well as vanity.

Detect original from copy,
legitimate from counterfeit.

Are twins identical
or different in character,
gifts, and soul? Are clones?

Do opposites attract or likes,
like halves in The Symposium?

"[We were] like to a double cherry,
    seeming parted, / But yet an union in partition."
And what of figure and ground?
Of metaphor?

"[I'd give the world] to be
    to you translated."

Metaphors discover parallels
between disparate things;
or "their interaction creates
a new meaning," according to
I.A. Richards. Gregor Samsa,
lowly clerk, becomes the bug
he feels like. Fancy offends logic,
yet we inhabit the feeling.

And what of nonpareils,
beyond compare? Unparalleled?
Pure being as hyperbole?

A bug or a rose as what it is.
One of a kind or the last.

Performances

To (en)act, accomplish, deliver,
fulfill; or pretend to.

Measured by rubrics,
we out- or under-;
satisfy, exceed or fail.

Piece of cake,
or mission impossible;
personal bests,
our own and others'.

Or called to entertain,
by script or improv,
we train, practice and rehearse.
Lend voice to words,
breath and touch to instruments,
body's motion to music;
we're live or taped.

Only some arts are, whether
street, mob, or ticketed.
Some public, some private.
Some perfunctory or inspired.

Some are solitary.
e.g. the old man with
bones of his epic fish.
Does it ever count
if only self can know?

No compensating for
milady's scorn:
"you look but on a stool!"
Or Goneril's for Albany:
"Marry, your manhood, mew!"

Auditions for all, and
in time, many parts.
The lover, partner,
friend, father, son,
the editor, teacher, writer,
the human being, etc.

Grant me, please,
your indulgences, oh reader
and myself. The kinder we,
to take our efforts
in might, not merit.

Yet still the wonder!
"Let there be light."
Our world as stage.
Final and forever.

Generous

Opposed to stingy,
possessive, vicious,
or close-fisted. Liberal instead,
open-handed, bountiful, kind.

Gen, the prefix from Greek
means birth, race, or *kind*—
in its second sense of
humankind, species, kin—
and links generosity
to the notions of genitals,
generic, and generation.

Ancestors contributed
to the gene pool;
produced us as progeny.

*

King Lear, the play,
explores evil and its genesis.

The aged king
divides his kingdom
into thirds for three daughters,
expecting their gratitude;

yet banishes the youngest
and redivides her share
when she refuses to flatter.

Soon regrets his error.
The elder sisters
turn on him, like kites,
serpents, or wolves;

"being weak, seem so,"
    they warn him;
degenerates, he calls them.
Prays for their sterility.

        *

Jane Smiley, in her novel
A Thousand Acres,
(a feminist retelling),

imagines her Lear
as an Iowa farmer
and the prime degenerate,
who has sexually abused
the older sisters
before the third was born.

        *

Perhaps the youngest
isn't Lear's at all.

*

Both dismissing and
cast from court,
and accompanied only
by his fool and (later)
the loyal Kent (in disguise)
Shakespeare's Lear fights
inner/outer weather.
Calls for doomsday. Blames
elements for conspiring
with his daughters.

Progresses from self-pity
to pity for fools,
madmen and beggars;
all wretches he's overlooked
with privileged indifference.

"Is man no more than this?"
Disrobes. Becomes collectivist.

In madness reasons
on hypocrisy of pomp.
Which is judge, or thief?
Since all are guilty,
"None does offend."

Finds sleep and is awoken
by his youngest, now
Queen of France,

who has invaded England
to rescue him. Ashamed,
he tries to kneel. Touches
her tears. Apologizes,
since she has cause to blame,
but she repeats: "no cause."

Yet, her army loses.
She and Lear are imprisoned.
Lear vows nothing
can ever part them; they'll
spend their time rehearsing
their reunion, and reflect on
the "mystery of things,"
like "God's spies" or like
mortal audiences at a play.

*

Still we're wrenched
by Act V, when she is hung.
One older sister kills the other,
then commits suicide.
And Lear, released and
howling like an animal,
carries in his youngest.
Lays her down, bends close.
Asks for mirror and feather,
imagines feather stirs,
then sees it doesn't.

Dies himself, apparently
amazed at miracle, injustice,
and maybe, something more:
"Look there, look there!"

*

Gen. Genius, we say.

*

However, Shakespeare's
Act V seemed ungenerous,
if not immoral,
to Samuel Johnson.

John Keats, rereading Lear,
aspired to its "negative capability."

Tolstoy hated the play. Freud
read it as a myth about
accepting mortality.

A.C. Bradley read it
like a Dostoyevski novel,
"too huge for the stage,"
and stressed its Christian morality.

Post-Holocaust and Cold War,
Jan Kott's existential reading
preceded Grigori Kozintsky's stark film
(soon rivaled by Peter Brook's).

Wisest and most congenial
is Maynard Mack's reminder:
"Tragedy never tells us what to think;
it shows us what we are and may be."

*

"Gentle Shakespeare," Ben Jonson wrote.
The cruelest truths can be kind.

PART FOUR

Fun

Eeyore beats Tigger
at Poohsticks, letting his stick drop
"in a twitchy sort of way."
Killjoy? Joystick? Joie de vivre.
"In the meantime, in between time,
ain't we got fun?"

Take a break. Relax! Lighten up!
"A temporary interruption
of ordinary life." Let down your hair.
Forget yourself. Be a sport.
Puppy, go fetch! Funny bone.
Make fun (at whose expense)?
Play pranks. Join in.
Just funning. Having fun.
Don't be a wet blanket.
Fiddle while Rome burns.
Satanic laughter.
The shadow knows.
"Ask for me tomorrow, and
you shall find me a grave man."

Tickling and being tickled.
Torments of delight. Slapstick. Pratfalls.
Flirt with disaster, as if immune.
Bounce back. Moonwalk. Near misses.
Funhouse distortions and scares.
The Absurd. Incongruity, reversals.
Sitcom (all plot); self-com (character driven).
Jester, mocker, puppeteer.
"Lord, what fools these mortals be."

Sudden glory. Have a ball!
Amusement Park! "Patch" Adams's
Gesundheit! Institute!

Beware lest jokes go lame or flat.
Don't lay an egg.
"What, is it time to jest and dally now?"
Jokes that need to be explained
go over like a lead balloon.
Laughable errors
elide to crimes and worse.

Can anyone suppress our
"eternal child"?
We chuckle, chortle, snicker, snort,
guffaw and shriek, slap knees, stamp feet,
convulse until we weep.

Endorphins promote health.
Don't worry, you'll laugh about it later.
Laugh it off. Laugh last.

P.S. If the offer seems
"funny" (meaning wrong),
don't bite... an afterlife, for
instance, where choirs of
angels, harmonies and
heavenly delights
don't sound much fun.

Games

Ludology: the Study of Games. *Ludicrous*:
Silly, Playful. *Magister Ludi.*

Games of chance and skill.
Of brain and brawn, mind and body.
Disciplines called sports.
Competitions for prizes, each
with rules, goals and stakes.

For amusement, escape, or exercise.
To teach life skills, especially war.
To educate. Diversions for the idle.
Child's play. Animal play: go fetch!

Bridge or poker. Parlor charades.
Game shows on TV. Blood sports.
Gladiators fight to death. Christians and lions.
The most dangerous game:
human hunter versus human quarry
(or fair game). Hunger games.
Bergman's Knight plays chess against Death.
Let the games begin!

"The only response / To a child's grave is /
to lie down before it and play dead,"
wrote the playful poet Bill Knott.
Of course, Knott himself played dead
in protest of the Viet Nam war, proclaiming
his later work to be posthumous.

Get serious. Stop fooling around.
I'm tired of all your games.
I'm not playing, I'm serious!

Players. Play-boy/-mate. Dating game.
Games aren't for keeps, or are they?
In French, a gamine means a young woman,
playful and sexually appealing
(the feminine form of gamin
meaning urchin, waif,
or playful, naughty child).

Fun and games. Out-of-luck Rosalind
when urged to be merry by her cousin, vows:
"From henceforth, I will, coz, and devise sports,"
such as falling in love. Coz cautions:
"Prithee do, to make sport withal,
but love no man in good earnest, nor go
further in sport neither than with safety
of a pure blush, thou mayst in honor
come off again." Roz directly falls
for a wrestler at first sight.

The cakes and ale gang pranks
Malvolio. Supposes. Practices.
Jests. Practical jokes. No fun for butts.
I'll be revenged on the whole pack of you.

No fair cheating. Rosie Luis jumps
in at the end of the Boston Marathon.
Rigged games for suckers.

I'm game. She's got game.
What's your game, i.e. racket?
Games where everybody wins.
Zero sum games. Nobody wins.

Game over.

The Birdly

The "full-body flight simulator"
has a tilt-able bench like an
examination table.

Lower yourself to knee pads,
lie spread-eagle with arms and hands
on flappable paddles.
Fit on VR goggles, raise face to fan,
get strapped in; and you're flying!

Lean left and dip, flap arms
and climb, raise palms and slow.
Dive, swoop. Feel wind.
See feathered wing-tips in periphery.

All around, the fading horizon;
below, a cityscape, the drop,
the tops of jagged high-rises,
geometric, man-made, which
shrink or loom; the grid of streets.

You're free within a 3D space,
cartoonish, yet "immersive";
the wind and pumping arms for touch,
the smells of ozone or pollution,
ocean, open fields and forests,
plunging speed or hovering.

It's past the size of dreaming.
Past memory, metaphor, analogy...
Icarus's melting wax.

Flight ends by crash
or power switch. Fan stills.

Unfeathered bipeds,
goggle free, unstrapped,
we welcome weight.
Our world is no cartoon.

Jerks

That chiseler in the traffic jam.
Three lanes immobile, motors revving,
heat shimmering, cars barely rolling,
lines stretching out of vision.
While on the other side, of course,
traffic snaps and whizzes past.

That guy or lady, that Archie Bunker
or teen babe in a red Subaru
convertible, roof down, cell to ear,
who pulls out suddenly from behind,
accelerates up the breakdown lane,
sets an example for other jerks,
one, two, five, ten. Up ahead
they chisel back. Never
are they punished (you fume).
No cops. No irate citizens stone-walling,
forcing them to wait stalled, while
those who have waited as they should,
those who played by the rules, inch by inch,
creep by toward gradual restorations
of freedom, progress, destinations.

No. Jerks through uncaring and audacity
get away with being jerks. Even feel superior
(you can tell from their jerk smirks).

They barge back in where they need.
Intimidate citizen Jones there,
who tries to stone-wall, tries to keep close
just as jerk honks, jerk grapples for eye contact,
jerk edges pristine paint-job and bumper
(or maybe edges junker with nothing-to-lose bumper)
against the citizen's bumper, daring to dare --
go on, run into me, I'm barging in
another inch or two, brake now,
give room or we scrape. There, see.
You blinked. Whistling, perhaps flipping the bird,
jerk rolls into line while you brake.
Jerk!!! Jerk!!! Chiseler!!!

Maybe you, citizen, should be a jerk.
Jerks get where they are going.
You, citizen, what about you?
Handy, dandy, where's the jerk?
Conformists. Sheep. All of you, all of us,
boiling out our radiators. Spending our day,
our days, our lives in cooperative stasis.

Maybe. Why not? Hell.
Check car behind. Watch the surge
of other chiselers, pulling out, rolling by,
mocking the folly of the law abiding.
Abiding! you sneer. Abiding! Lunacy. Now!
Your break, your instant to intimidate!

Force your way into breakdown lane,
accelerate. Pass the cars
you've watched for trancelike,
numbing, seething hours, when the one
you tail hits brakes, slows.

You're jammed with jerks, the renegades,
the take-it-into-their-own-handers.

Your illegal lane stops dead.
Filled up. Over-subscribed.

And wouldn't you know, then, just then,
the abiding lane of citizens you left,
well, it is moving, however slowly.

That family man, that baldy
with his two-and-one-half kids, his singing wife,
he's been in your mirror all day. Now
as he passes, he laughs and points:
at you. YOU! You, jerk.

Gone Phishing

Scar-lipped, still I get hooked.
As I sign off Amazon, I'm asked to fill out
a customer survey in exchange for
a dress wrist-watch, free!—as long as
I give my credit card for $8 bucks S&H.

Too good to be true, but offer looks legit.
If no watch arrives, I'll report the merchant,
but one does! Two days later, a knock-off of
a Rolex, made in China. Nice strap, nice
sliding box. I show my wife. Since my
Casio is fine, maybe I'll offer this to
my son-in-law or friend.

                   Four weeks after this,
I receive a second watch. Their error?
First order filled twice? I find
the original $7.71 on my statement,
followed by another charge for $98.54
two weeks later, and still another
$98.54 just now.

                   Feeling mugged,
I alert my bank, which blocks any
future charges from "Shop Amazing, FL."
but for refunds, tells me try the merchant first.
Okay. I found a flier with the second watch,
listing a website, "funtimehomegoods.com,"
where, along with the free watch offer,
I discover their small-print disclaimer,
that by paying S&H with credit card,
the subscriber agrees to a monthly $98.54 charge
for goods, unless s/he cancels within two weeks
of receiving the first watch. News to me.

I call their number; wait on hold,
then email them and get the response: "once a dispute
has been filed, we must work with your card-issuing
bank to settle the dispute." My bank,
in turn, needs an online dispute form
by snail mail, along with any evidence,
which proves superfluous, since over-night
I also complain to the Better Business Bureau,
which contacts Fun Time, which then
emails me, yes, they'd found my order,
canceled my subscription, and refunded charges.
I can "keep the watches complimentary."

I was jubilant, though concerned for other suckers.
And who were these Fun Timers? An enterprising
Mom and Pop; or sketchy venture on a larger scale?
It made no sense unless they found "subscribers" who
one, never stopped the charges or monthly deliveries;
two, sold the marked up watches at a further markup.
(I imagine sidewalk grifters with
watches lining their overcoats).

                    Incidentally, I'll
send YOU either watch for just $25. Let me know.
Or both for $45! That should cover time and trouble.

On Bars

A.G. Bill Barr
should be disbarred
and/or spend time
behind bars or
drinking at them,
both earnest and glib.
doing biddings of
our worst President,
bar none.

For lack of Barack,
step up, be heard;
raise the bar of expectations.
Climb the barricades.
High jump, pole-jump:
clear the bar.
Cross the bar.

Nearly half of us
fear barbarian hordes,
beards and all (unless
us is them). Seek to
bar the gate, build barriers.
Keep us over barrels, where
barrels are meant for
storing and protecting,
e.g. over Niagara;
or for shooting fish,
or empty ones for noise.

The BAR man sights down
his ungainly weapon
(though Browning Automatic Rifle
has nothing to do with "baros,"
Greek for weight).
Bars of gold, candy, or soap.
Bars of music and rank.
Barcode. Bar-
gain. Crow, salad,
barbell and barometer.
Stars and bars forever.

Barbed. Barred.

Democracy amok.

PART FIVE

On Knowing

We know our nakedness,
feel shame. Our children
are born in pain. Our byte
of apple still teases us.
The eternal blazon is
forbidden to mortal ears.
The bourne from which
no traveller returns remains
the dream of faith and science.
Taboo. Pandora's box.
The slightest facts of which
would set our hair on end,
harrow our souls.
and drive us mad.
We aren't wired for it.
Our fuses would melt.
At least that's our fear.
There must be always something
beyond comprehending.
ETs with bigger brains,
A.I. exceeding its creators.
All we know is learned.

As adults, we protect children
from complexities
beyond the bedroom wall.
We graduate, we think, from one
stage to the next,
innocence to experience,
processing discoveries,
wading deeper, deeper still,
learning to survive.

Enlightenment, we think;
masters of our fate, empowered
to create or end, not only selves,
but all our kind, all other
kinds, this planet itself.
But answers? Only in our dreams.
We'll never know each other
or ourselves.

On Meaning

What's the meaning of this?
How dare you?

We meant to, but forgot;
meant well, but failed.
Another time, maybe?
Dream deferred.

A meaningful experience,
you say. Meaning what?

Opposite of empty, pointless,
futile. Waste of time. Boring.
Nonsensical. Indecipherable.

We had the experience, but missed
the meaning.

Some fear wasting time,
e.g Thoreau: "I didn't want to live
what was not life, living is so dear."

Others go well-wadded with stupidity,
for fear of tragedy, or siren songs

(Not all meanings are positive, of course.
Lessons in futility. Mistakes. Dead ends.
Reverse effects. Traumas.)

I'm going to get drunk! Or never again!
Suicide's not all it's stacked up to be.
Or not to be.

Consider Cleopatra's show,
making hungry
where most she satisfies.

Consider natural wonders.
You've got to go there ,
experience the experience.
Or, you can't. Kant.

The suburban skeptic
David Brooks, sits on a rock
in the Big Blackfoot River
"waiting for one of those perfect
moments when time stops,"
but nothing happens.
Too late in the year, perhaps.

Landscapes, vistas.
Powers breathe forth.
My brother called the Rockies
God's Country.

Are you important? Necessary.
Useful. All you are meant to be?
To whom? To anyone?
To society? To yourself?

Room for five in the lifeboat.
Women and children first.

Who goes to combat?
Who stays home?
Essential personnel?

Glad you have self esteem, but
you don't mean anything to me.

What connections matter
and what don't?
Oh, that was just sex.

Tennis without a net.
Golf without a money bet.
Poetry, utilitarians think.

The Torture Machine's message
only gibberish still.

On Mirrors

My window, your reflection;
one-way spies on privacy.
Narcissus drowned
in self-love. Magic's judge
of beauty contest. Infant's
first wonder at her or his outside
seen while inside lived.
My right is left. Letters reversed.
Marx Bros. classic routine
from 1933's "Duck Soup".
(Harpo disguised as Groucho
mimes every Groucho move,
face-to-face in open doorway.)
Vampire's empty. Mourner's draped.
Self-portrait in a convex.

"Infinity effect" dizzies me
from the barber's chair, where I face
my reflection reflected in
the wall mirror behind me;
images in images repeat, recede.

Hall of. Step through to marvels
of illogic and nightmare.

Rear and sideview for
backing up or faring forward
while checking for pursuit.
(My parents' goodbye waves
as I returned to college.)

Cocaine dispenser. If broken,
seven years' bad luck.

Guidebook for magistrates.
Hold up to nature for poets.

Smoke and mirrors, we say.
Mirage or miracle to admire?

Deformed Richard III:
"I'll be at charges for a looking glass…
That I may see my shadow as I
pass." (Either I'm more handsome than I
thought, or noble women stupider and
weak.)

Deposed Richard II:
"Command a mirror hither straight
That it may show me what a face I have
Since it is bankrupt after majesty."
(I only know myself as rightful king;
I can't imagine myself as less.)

And so, for selves and souls in time,
both searching and unrecognized.

May mirror neurons fire.

On Skin

In the game.
Rhinoceros for thickest.
Smooth and softest:
infant cheeks.

To skin is to flay,
as St. Bartholomew does the artist
on the Sistine Chapel fresco;
holding up his pelt, with features
run down, limp in folds.

Hairless, scaleless and vulnerable
we kill and flay animals for hides,
make blankets, coats, shelters,
drums, shoes, belts, purses,
parchment, rugs, and wall hangings.

Once ermine-robed
in Gerald David's painting,
"The Judgment of Cambyses" (ca. 1500).
a suborned judge is stripped,
tied down, and skinned alive.
Four separate flayers work
(a fifth pulls the left arm taut)
at King Cambyses's command.
The seat for the next judge
will be woven from the skin.

Centuries later, Nazis
adopted Swift's "Modest Proposal":
human skin for lampshades.

For discipline, give a good hiding.
Sure saved my skin!
Live in your own, or jump out of.
Uncomfortable in yours?
Differences only skin deep.

"I got you under my skin...
deep in the heart of me."

Or here, inked on my bicep
for daws to peck at.

Tattoos, once mainly for
sailors, bikers, skinheads,
and side-show ladies,
at least in Main Street minds,
or for occasional exotics
from different cultures,
are now popular for Millennials.

Conversation starters, slogans,
and body art: if we can't choose
our skins, let's decorate and
personalize. Bare your story,
and truly denote yourself.
What's the skinny on that one?
It only hurts for a moment,
lasts forever; and removal by laser
is an emerging enterprise.

Baby or babe in birthday suit
on bearskin rug. Skin on skin.

Skin tight—dress or bathing suit.
Like second skin. Frogman. Selkie.
Skinny dipping. Skin trade.
Foreskin: call the Mohel to cut.

Sun screen to protect from
sunburn, blisters, and cancer.
Tan lines. Freeze burn. Frost bite.
Burn victims need grafts.
Healthy vs. problem.
Teen skin plagued by acne.
Elders' prone to scars, creases,
sags, tags, and face lifts.

MRIs and x-ray vision.

We bought our children
"the visible woman,"
an anatomical model kit.
Its clear plastic shell joined
front and back, but first you
had to fit in skull and skeleton,
then all the vitals,
like puzzle pieces.
Only my surgeon brother
could get it right.

As for skin privileges,
prejudices, and profiling:
we're all mixed, passing.

Otherwise smoked windows,
hoodies, avatars, machine voices
or disembodied words
free us to reveal our depths.

Funky Robot

—in memory of James Alan McPherson

Can't tell the dancer
from the dance?

Why, there I am...
rustier than the tin man,
but game and trying.

For my wife, daughter,
guests and granddaughters,
I make jerky motions to the beat.

"This is called the Funky Robot,
taught to me by James McPherson
(author of 'Why I Love Country Dancing')
in Iowa," I say.

*

At ten I learned the box step
at Mrs. Hill's School of Dance.
Right hand open on her rounded back.
One...two, three; one...two, three.
Glide, don't step.

Her stale smell mixed with talc.
And then with girls my age,
taller than me, flat-chested.

*

At make-out parties,
we swayed, embracing,
and at proms, our chaperones
insisted on a gap.

Rock and roll or
crooner's ballads?
We studied TV's Bandstand.

*

In college, I never mastered jitterbug.
In grad school, however,
dances changed from Twist to Frug,
to free-for-alls of Soul.

I never knew what craze was in:
the Loco-Motion, Watusi, Mash Potato,
Monkey, Shimmy, Swim, or Boogaloo.

I evolved my own routine,
swiveled my hips as if hula hooping,
then snapped my fingers, did sidesteps.
Party-mates tried to follow:
"Oh, teach me that! Hey, look at this!"

*

I met Connie, a B.U. senior,
at an older writer's party.
We grooved at first dance.

Living together, we swayed
on creaking floorboards
(like slow dance)
as I proposed and she accepted.

Once married with children.
however, we rarely
danced as a couple.

We had family occasions on her side.
weddings, bar and bat mitzvahs.
She had fundraising dances
at the K through 6 school
where she taught, but besides
having back problems,
I felt reserved. My dancing days
were done. She danced
with other women while I watched.

*

By the Eighties, "social dancing"
had become partnerless,
a stoned frenzy of aloneness together.

*

We were childrearing, teaching,
with separate friends,
hers local parents and colleagues,
mine writers I admired
as I helped to start a literary magazine,
which led to travel and editor gigs
and the annual convention
of the Associated Writing Programs,
where, after three days of readings,
panels, and a book fair:

writers danced!

Writers were hip and sensual!
Except they tried too hard,
bodies less their element than words.

*

Running was my dance,
I thought. Marathon training.
Along the river in the Boston.
Rhythm of my heartbeat.
Grace in body's pace.

*

"Ladies, dancers don't have periods,"
a woman dancer once wrote.

But for runners, well, there's Uta Peppig,
cresting Heartbreak Hill with
blood on legs and mouthing "I can't!"
but going on to win.

*

"Do the hucklebuck.
If you don't know how to do it,
boy you're out of luck."

*

Besides "The Tin Man's Dance"
from The Wizard of Oz, McPherson was likely thinking of
young Michael Jackson's
robot dance during the Jackson-5's
performance of "Dancing Machine,"
in the Sixties.

He was also mocking
the white stereotype of
African-Americans having
natural rhythm, except for him.
"The square dance is
the only dance form
I ever mastered," he wrote.

Supposedly jerky, rather than supple,
at least before AI, microchips,
and MIT's Robotics Lab,
robots couldn't jump or dance,
even to electro funk.

*

True dancers, of course,
train for artificial naturalness.
"Light on her feet." The illusion
of ease depends on
practice, exercise, and toil
as well as on such gifts as
youth, litheness, stamina,
and coordination. They ask,
then grant their bodies to perform.

Meanwhile, most of us
most of the time, carry
ourselves as burdens;
badly jointed, painful to watch.
Don't got rhythm. Out of step.
Dreams confined within
the body's cage.

*

How much of marriage
follows your steps, mine, or ours?
How much needs to?

*

When a friend,
newly divorced and retired,
got fixed up with the widow
of a famous hoofer,
their date didn't go well.

"Hard shoes to fill," he quipped.

*

My oldest brother's widow
sent me a list of things
"You never knew about him":
such as, while suffering from COPD,
he took ballroom dance
lessons with his wife.

My second brother, a doctor,
visited my mother after
she quit her life-preserving meds.
They'd shared a last waltz,
until her heart monitor
had fallen off, causing nurses
to rush in, expecting the worst.

*

"Do we keep dancing because to stop
would mean the extinction of
everything we value?...or because
there are still things to celebrate?"
asks the Oedipus scholar, Claire Catenaccio,
about the ancient, tragic choruses.

PART SIX

Settling Scores

At odds. Getting even.
Eye for eye. Teach a lesson.
Tit for tat. Old wrongs "nursed."
Resentments, envies, injuries.
Cost to me, benefit to you.
Your advantage, my expense.

"Two households both alike in dignity...
from ancient grudge break to new mutiny."

In Shylock's case, the grudge
is more specific. The Christian merchant
"hates our sacred nation"; spits upon
his Jewish gaberdine, yet
seeks his cash for love.

Shylock blames the Christians
for his daughter's betrayal—
rather than strict parenting.

One scapegoat threatens another.
"If you prick us, do we not bleed?"

*

Prods and Papes in Belfast.
Debts and debtors. Satisfaction.
Equity and reckonings.

"You never let it go, do you?"
(my father to my mother
after decades in recovery.)
Bitter mercies.

*

Vengeance is mine, sayeth the Lord;
For Buddists: bad Karma.

*

"We're not enemies, we're rivals,"
a campus colleague warned me
about opposing his tenure.

"Give me your best shot,
but then watch out,
because I'm giving it back.
This is my life I'm fighting for."

*

Solomon's parable
of dividing a baby
claimed by two mothers.
Who loved it most?
The one who yielded
so it would live.

*

Break a butterfly upon the wheel.
Justify the ways of God to man.
A writer's quarrel with the world.
For wound, the bow of art.

Yet morality in the novel means
keeping your thumb off the scales.

Size Matters

Samuel Johnson condescended
to Swift's writing about size:

"When once you have thought of
 big men and little men,
 it is very easy to do all the rest,"
he told biographer Boswell.

He couldn't finish Gulliver's Travels,
which stands on the shoulders
of Homer's Odyssey,
with giants and gods in human form,
the Bible's David and Goliath,
Anglo Saxon's Beowulf, Nordic myths.

Having towered over Lilliputians,
Gulliver next visits Brobdingnag,
where he seems miniature.
Where the prurience of power frees

the Queen's humungous ladies-
in-waiting to play with him
like a harmless Ken-doll.

The handsomest at sixteen,
"would sometimes set me astride
 one of her nipples, with many other tricks.
 wherein the reader will excuse me
 for being over particular."

Brothers Grimm gave us Jack and the Beanstalk
and Goldilocks and Three Bears.
Aristocrats and peasants.

Darwin's evolution contributed issues
of brain size, inferior species and advanced,
natural selection and missing links,
followed by Freud's describing issues
of infant helplessness and
adult powers and control.

Post-Thomas E. Edison, Hollywood
offered images "bigger than life,"
with sounds and special effects
more powerful than words.

We get King Kong the puppet,
a sculpted head with a man inside
pulling levers to drop its jaw
and roll its eyes. A separate
sculpted paw as well, large
enough to hold Faye Wray.

And then in close-ups,
stop-frame shots to animate
a flexible, table-top figure,
covered in rabbit fur.

Love at first sight,
the blonde, white and
dress-skinned, screams and arches;

and Kong, well, male and curious,
sniffs, tickles, and peels this novelty,
too strange to break or eat;
until distracted by a pterodactyl... .

Remember the rest?
Enslaved in due course,
and brought back alive, Kong
escapes to roam Manhattan,
trains replace giant snakes,
sky-scrapers, cliffs; air-force fighters,
birds of prey: but all controlled
by creatures of Wray's size and breed.

Kong's fall from the Empire State
building is tragic, critics say.
He dies protecting Wray, who, in turn,
is traumatized, and unlikely ever
to settle for Bruce Cabot.

Exposing our monstrosities may be easy.
Down with: Speciesism. Sexism,
Racism. Classism. Materialism.
Greed, Sin and Psychoses. Environmental hubris.

But Hollywood has found its prey,
and projects its tropes
on both small screens and huge.

Souls know neither species nor scale.
Or so we wish and fantasize.

Girl In The Hairy Paw

Membrane loose,
legs pale beneath.

Like scabs or blisters
from my hand,
or peeling from my feet.

Like cast-off skins
from slither kinds,
and yet so different!
Not leaf, or rind.

I peel from shoulder.
Sniff a musky,
flower scent.

Hers: dazzling
behind eyes.

So soft to touch.
Still breathing.

Eyes wide. Head rolls.
Sees me up close.
Whimpers, kicks.
Curls and clenches
in my gentlest grip.

Lift closer for sniff.
Scent tickles,
like sap.

I tease with
gentlest strokes.
She gasps and fights.
Again, I stroke.
Her heat and soft,
her yellow fluff.
Wild pulsing
of her little life.
The panic of
sharp cries.

And on my finger,
faint from long ago,
I'm breathing in
my Momma's musk.

Celebration of Food

My Australian friend wrote
"An Ode to Neenish Tarts,"
to celebrate her local pastry,
with its yin/yang
chocolate icing and jam filling;
but also, perhaps, to celebrate "tarts"
as complicated women.

While cannibals may eat their kind,
even vegans tease
each other's appetites
of body, soul, and mind.

Hungering, we look into
our meals as if beloved.
Salivate over a real dish.

Condemned man's wish
for final meal (imagination fails):
how about a Big Mac?

I recall my mother's roast beef,
the charred outside with spices
and juice. The smell of its roasting.
Pink within. Roast potatoes,
glazed with gravy.

(Also foods that made me gag:
cabbage, sauerkraut, lima beans.
Brussel sprouts. Asparagus.
Cauliflower. No baked beans,
thanks, mixed with hot dogs.
No fish, except tuna with
mayonnaise. I hated little bones.)

Nutrition or entertainment?
Junk-food plays on weaknesses;
love for sugar, salt, and fat.
Our taste buds tuned to blare.

My sister with thyroid issues
in later-life was put on meds
that deadened taste.
Her only pleasure was
the crunch of celery, textures
probed with tongue.

The chef's piece de resistance
demands tantric concentration
to savor different ingredients
and how they contrast and blend:
sweet, salty, sour, bitter, and umami.

From gourmands to gluttons,
we revel in tastes. Except for
whole food dieters, who avoid
ultra-processed foods and rely on
fruits, vegetables, vitamins,
lean protein, minerals and fiber,
to ensure healthier, longer lives.

Speaking of which, my father,
a candy manufacturer,
over-sampled his own wares
and suffered from alcoholism,
diabetes, and obesity. He died at 72.

"Candy is delicious food;
  have some every day" changed
  to "Candy is a Fighting Food"
  as our company's slogan
  during World War 2. Sugar
  was rationed, but Candy qualified
  as an essential industry and survived
  on Army contracts for C-rations.

—A brief digression, I admit,
  from pastries, appetites, and wit.

What are you eating? My friend
  private-messages me during the
  poetry zoom she co-hosts,
  which spans my Boston dinner hour
  and ends before her breakfast.

On Energy

Mass times speed of light
squared. Neither created
nor destroyed. Electro-magnetic
or nuclear. Renewable
or carbon-based.

Harnessing the elements.
Industry by waterwheel.
Wind farms at sea and land.
Solar panels any-/everywhere.

Splitting atoms to boil water
for steam turbines, replacing
boilers stoked by coal,
oil, gas, or wood.

Horse power, feeling oats.
Gas-guzzler's pistons
and drive shaft.

Generator's magnet rotating
inside another magnet's field.
Conductors for AC or DC.

Conserve, store, or waste.
Batteries recharged.

*

Bodies and thought
burn fuel as well:
calories consumed
or stored as fat.

As for souls and hearts:
may Force be with you.
Positive Chi. Channeling.
Samson's strength
from hair and prayer.

Inspired by gods, muses,
or scornful lovers.
Driven by emotions.
Believed or shamed into powers
beyond ourselves.

Cheered on. Carried away.
Graced. Gifted. Possessed.
Don't know what got into me.
Adrenalin rush.
Furious or terrified.

*

Take a break. Have a breather.
Re-fuel. Re-charge. Re-vive.
Pick yourself up. Try again.

Jujitsu: harness the force
used against you. Tensile:
bent bow; stretched or depressed spring.
Bungee cord tether. Bounce back.

Ambition. Envy. Kill or cheat.
Anticipation makes me wait.
Appetite or apathy.

Or serving others.
Making differences.
Wind at backs. Go with flow.
Joy of movement. Common cause.
Strength of conviction. Invictus!

*

Henry Adams in 1900
preferred goddesses to
dynamos: "All the steam
in the world could not,
like the Virgin, build Chartres."

Can't lift a finger.
Who cares about position
or condition in the world?
Accidia: one of the deadliest.

Duration

Dura-cell or Ever-ready?
From Latin durare, "to last."

We endure boredom, pain, hardships.
Eyes shut, I wait
for the dentist's drill to stop.

Fleeting pleasures.
Height exceeds length.

Troilus waits for Cressida's return.
We follow every "detail of
the prolonged and sickening
process to despair…"
wrote C.S. Lewis.
"No one without reluctance
reads it twice."

We hope for durability
of spirit and of goods.

We prize sustainability,
at least until we grow
careless and complacent.

One night stand
or golden anniversary.
Constancy, friendship,
wounds healed.
We serve for the duration.

Held breath or stretched note.
Obdurate, we won't yield.

Durance is punishment.
They gave him life, no parole.

Anticipation makes me wait.
Spans long or brief for art, for life.
No motion is perpetual.

Andrew Wyeth

Walking north, while traffic passed,
I saw from Bridge Street bridge
upstream, where the current hits rocks
and broken concrete from blocks
that once held waterwheels for the
brick-walled mills on opposite banks,
how midday sun struck a lower casement
on the far building, which reflected its image,
distinct as a photograph, bright on
the dark spill, foam and rush,
where the current swirled back,
a counter wave, and the main
flow kept straight and under the bridge.
All that drama! Commotion!
Vivid yellows, reds, browns, brick,
reeds, grasses (a quiet pool below
to my left, where two geese paddled),
turquoise sky, green, swift and constant
flow, the image of the window
projected, complete with silhouette
of a tree branch, like a carpet,
floating, fixed. I paused to let
these marvels register; then kept on
in my crossing, heading home.
Even time of day was part,
fall into winter. Eterne in mutability.
One more canvas Andrew Wyeth failed
to capture, paint, and frame.

The Singer

I walk the wooded MDC
bike path either down
the north bank of the Charles
towards Boston,
then cross the bridge
at Watertown Square and return
on the southern path;
or vice versa for variety.
Home and back takes an hour.

Once used mainly by joggers
and bikers, now since
apartment complexes have
replaced the backs of deserted
factories and commercial lots,
the path attracts all sorts.

The river is its own attraction.
Some locals fish from midstream
in hip-waders; sometimes kayakers
will lay in from the dam upstream,
then portage around our dam
just before the Square.
Still no swimming allowed,
after years of fighting pollution.

Squirrels, rabbits, snapping turtles
and song birds inhabit the shores,
while ducks, gabbling geese,
a pair of swans, and the rare blue heron
fly, swim, and feed in the water.
Flocks of seagulls fly inland
to fish, especially at the dams.

People sit or muse on benches.

I walk usually eyes down, as if
absorbed in thought. As strangers
approach, I avoid direct looks,
leave each to his or her own.
They're just fellow walkers,
talking to each other, perhaps,
or on their cell-phones. Or
lost in music on earbuds.

I feel crowded by those
who only creep past
and those I take
long minutes to pass.
I smile at dogs on leashes
and babies in strollers.

On hot days, I savor the
corridor of shade, breezes,
glowing leaves and shifting light,
the rush of flowing water.

There's a stench
behind an animal hospital
where dogs bark,
as if crying for rescue,
while keepers shout them down,
or try to; their muffled clamor
carries for a distance.

Joggers approach
swiftly from behind.
Bicyclists call "on your left!"

On the south path, seniors
from a nursing home
gather in a clearing
with picnic tables and speak
Russian to each other,
or spread along the path,
shuffling with walkers.

Electric skateboards are a novelty,
teens riding like surfers,
arms crossed, faster than bikes.

*   *   *

One perfect day after rain,
I'm surprised by singing,
which seems to join my spirit
in response to fresh air,
trees, river, and sky.
The voice is human, a woman's.
Not a radio or iPhone.
Not rap chanted to a beat
(there is one regular

biker who races with rap
blaring from his handlebars,
a rude disturber of the peace),
but opera, which I don't usually
like, pure and outpouring.

I see the singer's back,
draw near, and pass, keeping
my pace, eyes down. She is Asian
and wears a silk kimono,
like a costume, and remains
absorbed in her song,
which continues unbroken.

Puccini, I think. The words
Italian. Her voice is trained,
perfectly modulated and pitched.
She must be rehearsing;
perhaps performs with
the Boston Opera Company.

Perhaps she lives nearby
or is on tour, visiting.

Her music fades behind me.

*   *   *

Back home, when I tell
my wife, she asks:
"Why didn't you stop
and compliment her?"

*   *   *

A week later, I overtake her,
still singing, but on the next
foot-bridge and behind the apartments.

She wears a floppy sunhat,
like a gardening hat, a white top,
shirt-tails out, baggy slacks,
and sneakers without socks.
She is thin, frail, and elderly,
though younger than me.
Her hair is white, tied back;
her face wrinkled. I stop
and make eye contact.

"Thank you. Your voice
is beautiful," I say. She seems
startled, then embarrassed;
then politely smiles
and nods. "Thank you,"
she says, as if unused to English.

I smile, turn and
leave her, out of respect.

I don't remember hearing
her voice resume behind me.

I've never found her since.

Rabbit

Regard the luckless cotton-tail,
cat-sized, brown fur, an adult survivor
from our river path or nearby woods.

While foraging in last week's blizzard,
which had emptied the mall's tarmac,
she'd been scooped into an avalanche
by a front-loading plow, smothered,
crushed, and lifted as it surged; then
dumped into a drift against
the chain-link fence. That's my guess.

I walked plowed streets
to the mall's gym; took a side street
between apartment buildings.
Along the fence a path was cleared;
and just before the pedestrian gate,
there: the rabbit hung down, street-side:

front paws and head grazing
snow-clotted earth, but hind quarters
jammed mall-side by the mesh.

It had managed to push through
a diamond-shaped opening six rows up
and hardly four fingers wide.

It looked alive, stretched down;
eyes bright, teeth bared, so close
to free; improbable contortionist.

Its squeeze was like a camel's
through the eye of a needle,
or like a second birth gone wrong.

Residents must avoid the sight,
unsure who should remove it.
Mall owners? Sanitation? Animal Control?
Someone has to clip and pry the wire,
or hack the back legs from its hips.

Meanwhile, the carcass hangs stiffly;
probably will keep for spring.

Awakenings

I think of lines from The Winter's Tale:
"they looked as they had heard of a world
ransomed, or one destroyed."

For days, weeks, months
I've followed TV news
of Russia's invasion of Ukraine.

Ukrainians share our
consumerism, Western apartment
complexes, brand stores, cars,
familiar winter hats, coats, and boots,
pets (loved but silly-looking dogs),
bundled babies, strollers,
backpacks and rolling suitcases.
Kyiv could be Boston.

Doomsday is conceivable.
The blasphemies revisited.

*

From my 1940's childhood,
I remember ration stamps,
victory gardens, sirens
(my father enforced blackouts
as an air raid warden), my brothers'
military play, newsreels at the movies;

and then in Cold War 1950s,
the elementary school drills
crouched in a basement lunchroom,
with Civil Defense canisters
of cheese stacked along walls.
At home, I worried about
venetian blinds blowing like razors
across my bed, and imagined
the steady air raid signal first,

then the flash over Philadelphia
and having ten seconds to prepare
for the shockwave.

*

Now overlays Never Again.

"All history is a palimpsest,
scraped clean and re-inscribed,"
thinks Orwell's Big Brother.

Mutual Assured Destruction,
Industrial-Military Complex,
Doomsday Clock, Domino Theory,
Korea, Bay of Pigs, Vietnam,
Bosnia, Syria, Israel's Iron Dome,
Non-proliferation Treaties:
all scraped clean.

We sit, deliberate, and watch,
as our nation and NATO send
only "defensive weapons,"
for fear of Putin's nuclear threats.

Invasion turns to genocide.
Meriupol is leveled like Dresden,
Hiroshima, or Nagasaki.

Our eyes blur.

*

My electrician neighbor comes and goes,
with his MAGA hat and backyard
flag flapping: "Fuck Biden."
His house is his bunker.

In her BU dorm ten miles away,
our 18-year-old granddaughter
works on an essay for her Humanities class,
comparing Job's deity to those of
Homer: where is Justice?

Her mother, our daughter,
lives up our street and readies
a gallery show of her works
protesting racism.

My son and his wife sleep late
as they visit from Hoboken.
Downstairs my wife
makes their daughter breakfast.

More than toddling now, she brings us
energy, speech, and curiosity, explores
our house for treasures.
Captures territory. Conquers hearts.

Acknowledgments

I would like to *thank* the following publications in which these poems first appeared:

"On Risk," "Rabbit" in *Plume*: Issue #134 October 2022

"Andrew Wyeth" in *The Banyan Review,* Issue 13/Winter 2022

"On Knowing" in *Ibbetson Street,* #51, July, 2022

"Gone Phishing" in *Blyden Square Review,* Summer, June, 2022

"On Drift" in *Wisconsin Review,* No. 52.1, Spring 2022

"Heads Up" in *Ibbetson Street,* #50, December 26, 2021

"On Bars" in *The New Verse News,* Monday, April 13, 2020

"Scars" in *Westerly,* Volume 68, Number 1, July 2023

"Awakenings" in *Consequence Forum*, June 9, 2023

"Pratfalls" in *Somerville Times*, August 16, 2023

"On Rocks" in *Axon: Creative Explorations*,
        Vol 12, No 1, June 2022

"Fun" in *Play: An Anthology of Microlit*, March, 2023
        editor, Cassandra Atherton, *Spineless Wonders Press*

"Medallion," "Andrew Wyeth"
        in *The Banyan Review,* May 2021

"The Real Thing," "On Jerks," "Funky Robot"
        in *Woven Tale Press*, Vol. XI, #5, October 1, 2023

"On Heart," "Birdly," "Masquers"
        in *Constellations: A Journal of Poetry and Fiction*,
        Uncertainty, Vol 12, Fall 2022.

DeWitt Henry

DeWitt Henry

Born in Wayne, PA. Radnor High School, 1959; A.B. Amherst College, 1963; M.A. in English, Harvard University, 1965; Ph.D. English, Harvard University, 1971; completed requirements for M.F.A. University of Iowa, 1968 (did not take the degree).

Founding editor of *Ploughshares* literary magazine, and active editor and director 1971-1995. Interim Director of *Ploughshares* 6/2007-10/2008. Professor Emeritus, Emerson College, 2016-present. Professor, Writing, Literature, and Publishing, Emerson College, 2006-2015; Associate Professor 1989 to 2006: hired as Assistant Professor 1983; Acting Chairperson 1987-8; Chairperson 1989-93.

DeWitt is also a contributing editor to *Solstice: A Magazine of Diverse Voices* (2013-) and to *The Woven Tale Press: Arts and Literary Journal* (2016-).

Also by DeWitt Henry

Fiction

THE MARRIAGE OF ANNA MAYE POTTS
New Edition with Foreword by Margot Livesey
Pierian Springs Press, Spring 2024
1st Edition, University of Tennessee Press, 2001
(Winner of the **Peter Taylor Prize for the Novel**)

FALLING: SIX STORIES
CreateSpace, 2016

Essays

SWEET MARJORAM: NOTES AND ESSAYS
Plume Editions / MadHat Press, 2018

Memoir

ENDINGS & BEGINNINGS: FAMILY ESSAYS
MadHat Press, 2021
(Long-listed for the **PEN/Diamonstein-Spielvogel Award
for the Art of the Essay**, 2022)

VISIONS OF A WAYNE CHILDHOOD
CreateSpace, 2012

SWEET DREAMS: A FAMILY HISTORY
Hidden River Press, 2011

SAFE SUICIDE: ESSAYS, NARRATIVES, AND MEDITATIONS
Red Hen Press, 2008

Poetry

TRIM RECKONINGS: POEMS
Pierian Springs Press, November 2023

FOUNDLINGS: FOUND POEMS FROM PROSE
New Edition with Notes, Sources & Full Color Artwork
Pierian Springs Press, October 2023

RESTLESS FOR WORDS: POEMS
Finishing Line Press, February 2023

FOUNDLINGS: FOUND POEMS FROM PROSE
Life Before Man/Gazebo Books, May 2022

Anthologies

SORROW'S COMPANY: WRITERS ON LOSS AND GRIEF
Beacon Press, 2001

**BREAKING INTO PRINT: EARLY STORIES AND INSIGHTS
INTO GETTING PUBLISHED; A PLOUGHSHARES ANTHOLOGY**
Beacon Press, 2000

FATHERING DAUGHTERS: REFLECTIONS BY MEN
(with James Alan McPherson)
Beacon Press 1998, pb. 1999

OTHER SIDES OF SILENCE: NEW FICTION FROM PLOUGHSHARES
Faber and Faber, 1993, o.p.

THE PLOUGHSHARES READER: NEW FICTION FOR THE 80s
(Winner **Third Annual Editors Book Award**)
Pushcart Press, 1984, NAL, 1985

Printed in the USA
CPSIA information can be obtained
at www.ICGtesting.com
LVHW090604231123
764668LV00026B/452/J